CAT POOP OR RABBIT POOP?

By Colin Matthews

Gareth Stevens
PUBLISHING

Please visit our website, www.garethstevens.com. For a free color catalog of all our high-quality books, call toll free 1-800-542-2595 or fax 1-877-542-2596.

Cataloging-in-Publication Data

Names: Matthews, Colin.
Title: Cat poop or rabbit poop? / Colin Matthews.
Description: New York : Gareth Stevens Publishing, 2020. | Series: The scoop on poop | Includes glossary and index.
Identifiers: ISBN 9781538233368 (pbk.) | ISBN 9781538229538 (library bound) | ISBN 9781538233375 (6pack)
Subjects: LCSH: Cats–Juvenile literature. | Rabbits–Juvenile literature. | Animal droppings–Juvenile literature.
Classification: LCC SF445.7 M378 2019 | DDC 636.8–dc23

Published in 2020 by
Gareth Stevens Publishing
111 East 14th Street, Suite 349
New York, NY 10003

Copyright © 2020 Gareth Stevens Publishing

Designer: Sarah Liddell
Editor: Therese Shea

Photo credits: Cover, p. 1 Andrew Park/Shutterstock.com; p. 5 Rose Marinelli/Shutterstock.com; p. 7 Stone36/Shutterstock.com; p. 9 Moji Foto/Shutterstock.com; p. 11 ajlatan/Shutterstock.com; p. 13 Paul Reeves Photography/Shutterstock.com; p. 15 Fiver, der Hellseher/Wikimedia Commons; p. 17 KanphotoSS/Shutterstock.com; p. 19 (rabbit poop) EvgenyPopov/Shutterstock.com; p. 19 (cat poop) Fleuraya/Shutterstock.com.

Printed in the United States of America

CPSIA compliance information: Batch #CS19GS: For further information contact Gareth Stevens, New York, New York at 1-800-542-2595.

CONTENTS

Boldface words appear in the glossary.

Mystery in the Park

You're playing in the park. Out of the corner of your eye, you see something run into the bushes. It may have been a cat . . . or could it have been a rabbit? Whatever it was, it's gone! But it left behind a clue—poop!

Carnivorous Cats

Learning about both cats and rabbits can help you find out which animal left that poop! Cats are **carnivores**. They have many **adaptations** that help them catch prey. Their eyes help them see at night. They have sharp claws and teeth, too.

Cover Up

A healthy cat's scat, or poop, is dark brown and looks like little logs or **nuggets**. It often smells bad because of the cat's meat **diet**. However, cat poop isn't easy to spot or smell. Cats like to bury it!

Cats bury their scat to hide the smell from predators or other animals they fear. Even house cats bury poop in their litter boxes. It's a way to tell their owners that they know who's in charge!

Hopping Herbivores

Rabbits live in many kinds of **habitats** around the world. There are more than 30 species, or kinds. All are herbivores. That means they eat plants—such as the grass in the park. They eat seeds, fruits, roots, and tree bark, too.

A Strange Snack

Rabbits do something strange to get as many **nutrients** from their food as possible. The first time food travels through a rabbit's **digestive system**, it comes out as a kind of poop that they eat! It's often called night droppings.

As night droppings pass through a rabbit's digestive system, more nutrients are removed. What's left comes out as hard, round scat. It isn't usually stinky, but rabbits make a lot of it. One rabbit makes over 100 bits of poop a day!

Whose Poop?

Which animal left the droppings? Look at the **evidence**. Cat poop is shaped like small logs or nuggets. It's stinky. Rabbit poop is shaped like little balls. It doesn't smell. Cats often hide their poop. Rabbits leave their scat in the open.

RABBIT POOP

CAT POOP

19

Now You Know!

The poop you saw wasn't smelly. It was dry and round. It wasn't hidden either. From all this, you know what you saw must have been a rabbit's poop. Next time you spot it, you'll know a rabbit is nearby!

EXAMINE THE EVIDENCE

	CAT	RABBIT
WHAT DOES ITS POOP LOOK LIKE?	BROWN LOGS OR NUGGETS	SMALL BROWN BALLS
DOES THE POOP SMELL?	YES	NO
WHERE DOES IT POOP?	ANYWHERE, BUT HIDES IT	ANYWHERE

IT WAS THE RABBIT'S POOP!

GLOSSARY

adaptation: a change in an animal that makes it better able to live in its surroundings

carnivore: an animal that eats meat

diet: the food an animal eats

digestive system: the body parts that break down food inside the body so that the body can use it

evidence: something which shows that something else is true

habitat: the natural place where an animal or plant lives

nugget: a solid lump

nutrient: something a living thing needs to grow and stay alive

FOR MORE INFORMATION

BOOKS

Foran, Jill. *Rabbit*. New York, NY: AV² by Weigl, 2015.

Gardeski, Christina Mia. *Cat Behavior*. North Mankato, MN: Capstone Press, 2017.

Gregory, Josh. *Rabbits*. New York, NY: Children's Press, 2017.

WEBSITES

Fun Cat Facts for Kids
www.sciencekids.co.nz/sciencefacts/animals/cat.html
Read some more awesome info about cats.

Interesting Facts About Rabbits
www.mspca.org/pet_resources/interesting-facts-about-rabbits/
There's much more to learn about these furry animals.

INDEX